CALDERON, THE COURTIER

CALDERON, THE COURTIER

EDWARD BULWER-LYTTON

WILDSIDE PRESS

CALDERON, THE COURTIER.

A TALE.

CHAPTER I.

THE ANTE-CHAMBER.

THE Tragi-Comedy of Court Intrigue, which had ever found its principal theatre in Spain since the accession of the House of Austria to the throne, was represented with singular complication of incident and brilliancy of performance during the reign of Philip the Third. That monarch, weak, indolent, and superstitious, left the reins of government in the hands of the Duke of Lerma. The Duke of Lerma, in his turn, mild, easy, ostentatious, and shamefully corrupt, resigned the authority he had thus received to Roderigo Calderon, an able and resolute upstart, whom nature and fortune seemed equally to favour and endow. But not more to his talents, which were great, than to the policy of religious persecution which he had supported and enforced, Roderigo Calderon owed his promotion. The king and the Inquisition had, some years before our story opens, resolved upon the general expulsion of the Moriscos,—the wealthiest, the most active, the most industrious portion of the population.

"I would sooner," said the bigoted king,—and his words were hallowed by the enthusiasm of the Church,— "depopulate my kingdom than suffer it to harbour a single infidel."

The Duke de Lerma entered into the scheme that lost to Spain many of her most valuable subjects, with the zeal of a pious Catholic expectant of the cardinal's hat, which he afterwards obtained. But to this scheme Calderon brought an energy, a decision, a vehemence, and sagacity of hatred that savoured more of personal vengeance than religious persecution. His perseverance in this good work established him firmly in the king's favour; and in this he was supported by the friendship not only of Lerma, but of Fray Louis de Aliaga, a renowned Jesuit, and confessor to the king. The disasters and distresses occasioned by this barbarous crusade, which crippled the royal revenues, and seriously injured the estates of the principal barons, from whose lands the industrious and intelligent Moriscos were expelled, ultimately concentred a deep and general hatred upon Calderon. But his extraordinary address and vigorous energies, his perfect mastery of the science of intrigue, not only sustained, but continued to augment, his power. Though the king was yet in the prime of middle age, his health was infirm and his life precarious. Calderon had contrived, while preserving the favour of the reigning monarch, to establish himself as the friend and companion of the heir apparent. In this, indeed, he had affected to yield to the policy of the king himself; for Philip the Third had a wholesome terror of the possible ambition of his son, who early evinced talents which might have been formidable but for passions which urged him into the most vicious pleasures and the most extravagant excesses. The craft of the king was satisfied by the device of placing about the person of the Infant one devoted to himself; nor did his conscience, pious as he was, revolt at the profligacy which his favourite was said to participate, and, perhaps, to encourage, since the less popular the prince, the more powerful the king.

But all this while there was formed a powerful cabal against both the Duke of Lerma and Don Roderigo Calderon in a quarter where it might least have been anticipated. The cardinal-duke, naturally anxious to cement and perpetuate his authority, had placed his son, the Duke d'Uzeda, in a post that gave him constant access to the monarch. The prospect of power made Uzeda eager to seize at once upon all its advantages; and it became the object of his life to supplant his

The Royal Palace, Madrid.

father. This would have been easy enough but for the genius
and vigilance of Calderon, whom he hated as a rival, disdained as an upstart, and dreaded as a foe. Philip was soon
aware of the contest between the two factions; but, in the
true spirit of Spanish kingcraft, he took care to play one
against the other. Nor could Calderon, powerful as he was,
dare openly to seek the ruin of Uzeda; while Uzeda, more
rash, and, perhaps, more ingenuous, entered into a thousand
plots for the downfall of the prime favourite.

The frequent missions, principally into Portugal, in which
of late Calderon had been employed, had allowed Uzeda to
encroach more and more upon the royal confidence; while the
very means which Don Roderigo had adopted to perpetuate
his influence, by attaching himself to the prince, necessarily
distracted his attention from the intrigues of his rival. Perhaps, indeed, the greatness of Calderon's abilities made him
too arrogantly despise the machinations of the duke, who,
though not without some capacities as a courtier, was wholly
incompetent to those duties of a minister on which he had set
his ambition and his grasp.

Such was the state of parties in the Court of Philip the
Third at the time in which we commence our narrative in the
ante-chamber of Don Roderigo Calderon.

"It is not to be endured!" said Don Felix de Castro, an old
noble, whose sharp features and diminutive stature proclaimed
the purity of his blood and the antiquity of his descent.

"Just three-quarters of an hour and five minutes have I
waited for audience to a fellow who would once have thought
himself honoured if I had ordered him to call my coach," said
Don Diego Sarmiento de Mendoza.

"Then, if it chafe you so much, gentlemen, why come you
here at all? I dare say Don Roderigo can dispense with your
attendance."

This was said bluntly by a young noble of good mien, whose
impetuous and irritable temperament betrayed itself by an
impatience of gesture and motion unusual amongst his coun-
trymen. Sometimes he walked, with uneven strides, to and
fro the apartments, unheeding the stately groups whom he

jostled, or the reproving looks that he attracted; sometimes
he paused abruptly, raised his eyes, muttered, twitched his
cloak, or played with his sword-knot; or, turning abruptly
round upon his solemn neighbours, as some remark on his
strange bearing struck his ear, brought the blood to many a
haughty cheek by his stern gaze of defiance and disdain. It
was easy to perceive that this personage belonged to the tribe
— rash, vain, and young — who are eager to take offence, and
to provoke quarrel. Nevertheless, the cavalier had noble and
great qualities. A stranger to courts, in the camp he was renowned for a chivalrous generosity and an extravagant valour,
that emulated the ancient heroes of Spanish romaunt and
song. His was a dawn that promised a hot noon and a glori-
ous eve. The name of this brave soldier was Martin Fonseca.
He was of an ancient but impoverished house, and related in
a remote degree to the Duke de Lerma. In his earliest youth
he had had cause to consider himself the heir to a wealthy
uncle on his mother's side; and with those expectations,
while still but a boy, he had been invited to court by the
cardinal-duke. Here, however, the rude and blunt sincerity
of his bearing had so greatly shocked the formal hypocrisies
of the court, and had more than once so seriously offended
the minister, that his powerful kinsman gave up all thought
of pushing Fonseca's fortunes at Madrid, and meditated some
plausible excuse for banishing him from court. At this time
the rich uncle, hitherto childless, married a second time, and
was blessed with an heir. It was no longer necessary to keep
terms with Don Martin; and he suddenly received an order
to join the army on the frontiers. Here his courage soon
distinguished him; but his honest nature still stood in the
way of his promotion. Several years elapsed, and his rise
had been infinitely slower than that of men not less inferior
to him in birth than merit. Some months since, he had repaired to Madrid to enforce his claims upon the government;
but instead of advancing his suit, he had contrived to effect a
serious breach with the cardinal, and been abruptly ordered
back to the camp. Once more he appeared at Madrid; but
this time it was not to plead desert and demand honours.

In any country but Spain under the reign of Philip the
Third, Martin Fonseca would have risen early to high fortunes. But, as we have said, his talents were not those of
the flatterer or the hypocrite; and it was a matter of astonishment to the calculators round him to see Don Martin Fonseca
in the anteroom of Roderigo Calderon, Count Oliva, Marquis
de Siete Iglesias, secretary to the King, and parasite and favourite of the Infant of Spain.

"Why come you here at all?" repeated the young soldier.

"Señor," answered Don Felix de Castro, with great gravity,
"we have business with Don Roderigo. Men of our station
must attend to the affairs of the State, no matter by whom
transacted."

"That is, you must crawl on your knees to ask for pensions
and governorships, and transact the affairs of the State by
putting your hands into its coffers."

"Señor!" growled Don Felix, angrily, as his hand played
with his sword-belt.

"Tush!" said the young man, scornfully turning on his
heel.

The folding-doors were thrown open, and all conversation
ceased at the entrance of Don Roderigo Calderon.

This remarkable personage had risen from the situation of
a confidential scribe to the Duke of Lerma to the nominal
rank of secretary to the king, — to the real station of auto-
crat of Spain. The birth of the favourite of fortune was ex-
ceedingly obscure. He had long affected to conceal it; but
when he found curiosity had proceeded into serious investi-
gation of his origin, he had suddenly appeared to make a virtue of necessity; proclaimed of his own accord that his father
was a common soldier of Valladolid, and even invited to
Madrid, and lodged in his own palace, his low-born progeni-
tor. This prudent frankness disarmed malevolence on the
score of birth. But when the old soldier died, rumours went
abroad that he had confessed on his death-bed that he was not
in any way related to Calderon; that he had submitted to an
imposture which secured to his old age so respectable and
luxurious an asylum; and that he knew not for what end

Calderon had forced upon him the honours of spurious par-
entship.   This tale, which, ridiculed by most, was yet believed by some, gave rise to darker reports concerning one on
whom the eyes of all Spain were fixed.   It was supposed that
he had some motive beyond that of shame at their meanness
to conceal his real origin and name.   What could be that
motive, if not the dread of discovery for some black and
criminal offence connected with his earlier youth, and for
which he feared the prosecution of the law?   They who affected most to watch his exterior averred that often, in his
gayest revels and proudest triumphs, his brow would lower,
his countenance change, and it was only by a visible and
painful effort that he could restore his mind to its self-pos-
session.   His career, which evinced an utter contempt for the
ordinary rules and scruples that curb even adventurers into a
seeming of honesty and virtue, appeared in some way to jus-
tify these reports.   But, at times, flashes of sudden and brilliant magnanimity broke forth to bewilder the curious, to
puzzle the examiners of human character, and to contrast the
general tenor of his ambitious and remorseless ascent to
power.   His genius was confessed by all; but it was a
genius that in no way promoted the interests of his country.   It served only to prop, defend, and advance himself; to
baffle difficulties; to defeat foes; to convert every accident,
every chance, into new stepping-stones in his course.   Whatever his birth, it was evident that he had received every advantage of education; and scholars extolled his learning and
boasted of his patronage.   While, more recently, if the daring
and wild excesses of the profligate prince were, on the one
hand, popularly imputed to the guidance of Calderon, and in-
creased the hatred generally conceived against him, so, on the
other hand, his influence over the future monarch seemed to
promise a new lease to his authority, and struck fear into the
councils of his foes.   In fact, the power of the upstart marquis appeared so firmly rooted, the career before him so splendid, that there were not wanted whisperers who, in addition
to his other crimes, ascribed to Roderigo Calderon the assist-
ance of the black art.   But the black art in which that subtle

courtier was a proficient is one that dispenses with necro-
mancy.   It was the art of devoting the highest intellect to
the most selfish purposes,— an art that thrives tolerably well
for a time in the great world!

He had been for several weeks absent from Madrid on a
secret mission; and to this, his first public levee on his return, thronged all the rank and chivalry of Spain.

The crowd gave way, as, with haughty air, in the maturity
of manhood, the Marquis de Siete Iglesias moved along.   He
disdained all accessories of dress to enhance the effect of his
singularly striking exterior.   His mantle and vest of black
cloth, made in the simplest fashion, were unadorned with the
jewels that then constituted the ordinary insignia of rank.
His hair, bright and glossy as the raven's plume, curled back
from the lofty and commanding brow, which, save by one
deep wrinkle between the eyes, was not only as white but
as smooth as marble.   His features were aquiline and regular;
and the deep olive of his complexion seemed pale and clear
when contrasted by the rich jet of the mustache and pointed
beard.   The lightness of his tall and slender but muscular
form made him appear younger than he was; and had it not
been for the supercilious and scornful arrogance of air which
so seldom characterizes gentle birth, Calderon might have
mingled with the loftiest magnates of Europe and seemed to
the observer the stateliest of the group.   It was one of those
rare forms that are made to command the one sex and fasci-
nate the other.   But, on a deeper scrutiny, the restlessness
of the brilliant eye, the quiver of the upper lip, a certain
abruptness of manner and speech, might have shown that
greatness had brought suspicion as well as pride.   The spectators beheld the huntsman on the height,— the huntsman
saw the abyss below, and respired with difficulty the air
above.

The courtiers one by one approached the marquis, who received them with very unequal courtesy.   To the common
herd he was sharp, dry, and bitter; to the great he was obsequious, yet with a certain grace and manliness of bearing
that elevated even the character of servility; and all the

while, as he bowed low to a Medina or a Guzman, there was a half imperceptible mockery lurking in the corners of his mouth, which seemed to imply that while his policy cringed, his heart despised.   To two or three, whom he either personally liked or honestly esteemed, he was familiar, but brief, in his address; to those whom he had cause to detest or to dread — his foes, his underminers — he assumed a yet greater frankness, mingled with the most caressing insinuation of voice and manner.

Apart from the herd, with folded arms, and an expression of countenance in which much admiration was blent with some curiosity and a little contempt, Don Martin Fonseca gazed upon the favourite.

"I have done this man a favour," thought he; "I have contributed towards his first rise,— I am now his suppliant. 'Faith! I, who have never found sincerity or gratitude in the camp, come to seek those hidden treasures at a court! Well, we are strange puppets, we mortals!"

Don Diego Sarmiento de Mendoza had just received the smiling salutation of Calderon, when the eye of the latter fell upon the handsome features of Fonseca.   The blood mounted to his brow; he hastily promised Don Diego all that he desired, and hurrying back through the crowd, retired to his private cabinet.   The levee was broken up.

As Fonseca, who had caught the glance of the secretary, and who drew no favourable omen from his sudden evanishment, slowly turned to depart with the rest, a young man, plainly dressed, touched him on the shoulder.

"You are Señor Don Martin Fonseca ?"

"The same."

"Follow me, if it please you, señor, to my master, Don Roderigo Calderon."

Fonseca's face brightened; he obeyed the summons; and in another moment he was in the cabinet of the Sejanus of Spain.

CHAPTER II.

THE LOVER AND THE CONFIDANT.

CALDERON received the young soldier at the door of his chamber with marked and almost affectionate respect.

"Don Martin," said he, and there seemed a touch of true feeling in the tremor of his rich sweet voice, "I owe you the greatest debt one man can incur to another,— it was your hand that set before my feet their first stepping-stone to power. I date my fortunes from the hour in which I was placed in your father's house as your preceptor. When the cardinal-duke invited you to Madrid, I was your companion; and when, afterwards, you joined the army, and required no longer the services of the peaceful scholar, you demanded of your illustrious kinsman the single favour,— to provide for Calderon. I had already been fortunate enough to win the countenance of the duke, and from that day my rise was rapid. Since then we have never met. Dare I hope that it is now in the power of Calderon to prove himself not ungrateful?"

"Yes," said Fonseca, eagerly; "it is in your power to save me from the most absolute wretchedness that can befall me. It is in your power — at least I think so — to render me the happiest of men!"

"Be seated, I pray you, señor. And how? I am your servant."

"Thou knowest," said Fonseca, "that, though the kinsman, I am not the favourite, of the Duke of Lerma?"

"Nay, nay," interrupted Calderon, softly, and with a bland smile; "you misunderstand my illustrious patron: he loves you, but not your indiscretions."

"Yes, honesty is very indiscreet! I cannot stoop to the life of the ante-chamber; I cannot, like the Duke of Lerma, detest my nearest relative if his shadow cross the line of my interests. I am of the race of Pelayo, not Oppas; and my profession, rather that of an ancient Persian than a modern Spaniard, is to manage the steed, to wield the sword, and to speak the truth."

There was an earnestness and gallantry in the young man's aspect, manner, and voice, as he thus spoke, which afforded the strongest contrast to the inscrutable brow and artificial softness of Calderon; and which, indeed, for the moment, occasioned that crafty and profound adventurer an involuntary feeling of self-humiliation.

"But," continued Fonseca, "let this pass: I come to my story and my request. Do you, or do you not know, that I have been for some time attached to Beatriz Coello?"

"Beatriz," repeated Calderon, abstractedly, with an altered countenance, "it is a sweet name,— it was my mother's!"

"Your mother's! I thought to have heard her name was Mary Sandalen?"

"True,— Mary Beatriz Sandalen," replied Calderon, indifferently. "But proceed. I heard, after your last visit to Madrid, when, owing to my own absence in Portugal, I was not fortunate enough to see you, that you had offended the duke by desiring an alliance unsuitable to your birth. Who, then, is this Beatriz Coello?"

"An orphan of humble origin and calling. In infancy she was left to the care of a woman who, I believe, had been her nurse; they were settled in Seville, and the old *gouvernante's* labours in embroidery maintained them both till Beatriz was fourteen. At that time the poor woman was disabled by a stroke of palsy from continuing her labours, and Beatriz, good child, yearning to repay the obligation she had received, in her turn sought to maintain her protectress. She possessed the gift of a voice wonderful for its sweetness. This gift came to the knowledge of the superintendent of the theatre at Seville: he made her the most advantageous proposals to enter upon the stage. Beatriz, innocent child, was unaware of the perils of that profession; she accepted eagerly the means that would give comfort to the declining life of her only friend,— she became an actress. At that time we were quartered in Seville, to keep guard on the suspected Moriscos."

"Ah, the hated infidels!" muttered Calderon, fiercely, through his teeth.

"I saw Beatriz, and loved her at first sight. I do not say," added Fonseca, with a blush, "that my suit at the outset was that which alone was worthy of her; but her virtue soon won my esteem as well as love. I left Seville to seek my father and obtain his consent to a marriage with Beatriz. You know a hidalgo's prejudices,— they are insuperable. Meanwhile, the fame of the beauty and voice of the young actress reached Madrid, and hither she was removed from Seville by royal command. To Madrid, then, I hastened, on the pretence of demanding promotion. You, as you have stated, were absent in Portugal on some State mission. I sought the Duke de Lerma. I implored him to give me some post, anywhere — I recked not beneath what sky, in the vast empire of Spain — in which, removed from the prejudices of birth and of class, and provided with other means, less precarious than those that depend on the sword, I might make Beatriz my wife. The polished duke was more inexorable than the stern hidalgo. I flew to Beatriz; I told her I had nothing but my heart and right hand to offer. She wept, and she refused me."

"Because you were not rich?"

"Shame on you, no! but because she would not consent to mar my fortunes, and banish me from my native land. The next day I received a peremptory order to rejoin the army, and with that order came a brevet of promotion. Lover though I be, I am a Spaniard; to have disobeyed the order would have been dishonour. Hope dawned upon me,— I might rise, I might become rich. We exchanged our vows of fidelity. I returned to the camp. We corresponded. At last her letters alarmed me. Through all her reserve, I saw that she was revolted by her profession, and terrified at the persecutions to which it exposed her; the old woman, her sole guide and companion, was dying; she was dejected and un-

happy; she despaired of our union; she expressed a desire
for the refuge of the cloister. At last came this letter, bid-
ding me farewell forever. Her relation was dead; and, with
the little money she had amassed, she had bought her entrance
into the convent of St. Mary of the White Sword. Imagine
my despair! I obtained leave of absence, I flew to Madrid.
Beatriz is already immured in that dreary asylum; she has
entered on her novitiate."

"Is that the letter you refer to?" said Calderon, extending
his hand.

Fonseca gave him the letter.

Hard and cold as Calderon's character had grown, there
was something in the tone of this letter — its pure and noble
sentiments, its innocence, its affection — that touched some
mystic chord in his heart. He sighed as he laid it down.

"You are, like all of us, Don Martin," said he, with a bit·
ter smile, "the dupe of a woman's faith. But you must purchase experience for yourself; and if, indeed, you ask my
services to procure you present bliss and future disappoint-
ment, those services are yours. It will not, I think, be diffi-
cult to interest the queen in your favour; leave me this letter,
— it is one to touch the heart of a woman. If we succeed
with the queen, who is the patroness of the convent, we may
be sure to obtain an order from court for the liberation of the
novice: the next step is one more arduous. It is not enough
to restore Beatriz to freedom, — we must reconcile your family
to the marriage. This cannot be done while she is not noble;
but letters patent [here Calderon smiled] could ennoble a
mushroom itself — your humble servant is an example. Such
letters may be bought or begged; I will undertake to procure
them. Your father, too, may find a dowry accompanying the
title, in the shape of a high and honourable post for yourself.
You deserve much; you are beloved in the army; you have
won a high name in the world. I take shame on myself that
your fortunes have been overlooked. 'Out of sight out of
mind;' alas! it is a true proverb. I confess that, when I
beheld you in the anteroom, I blushed for my past forgetful-
ness. No matter, — I will repair my fault. Men say that

my patronage is misapplied; I will prove the contrary by your promotion."

"Generous Calderon!" said Fonseca, falteringly; "I ever hated the judgments of the vulgar. They calumniate you; it is from envy."

"No," said Calderon, coldly; "I am bad enough, but I am still human. Besides, gratitude is my policy. I have always found that it is a good way to get on in the world to serve those who serve us."

"But the duke?"

"Fear not; I have an oil that will smooth all the billows on that surface. As for the letter, I say, leave it with me; I will show it to the queen. Let me see you again to-morrow."

————◆————

CHAPTER III.

A RIVAL.

CALDERON's eyes were fixed musingly on the door which closed on Fonseca's martial and noble form.

"Great contrasts among men!" said he, half aloud. "All the classes into which naturalists ever divided the animal world contain not the variety that exists between man and man. And yet we all agree in one object of our being, — all prey on each other! Glory, which is but the thirst of blood, makes yon soldier the tiger of his kind; other passions have made me the serpent: both fierce, relentless, unscrupulous, — both! hero and courtier, valour and craft! Hem! I will serve this young man, — he has served me. When all other affection was torn from me, he, then a boy, smiled on me and bade me love him. Why has he been so long forgotten? He is not of the race that I abhor, — no Moorish blood flows in his veins; neither is he of the great and powerful, whom I dread, nor of the crouching and the servile, whom I despise; he is one whom I can aid without a blush."

While Calderon thus soliloquized, the arras was lifted aside, and a cavalier, on whose cheek was the first down of manhood, entered the apartment.

"So, Roderigo, alone! welcome back to Madrid. Nay, seat thyself, man,— seat thyself."

Calderon bowed with the deepest reverence, and, placing a large *fauteuil* before the stranger, seated himself on a stool, at a little distance.

The new comer was of sallow complexion; his gorgeous dress sparkled with prodigal jewels. Boy as he was, there was yet a careless loftiness, a haughty ease, in the gesture,— the bend of the neck, the wave of the hand,— which, coupled with the almost servile homage of the arrogant favourite, would have convinced the most superficial observer that he was born of the highest rank. A second glance would have betrayed, in the full Austrian lip, the high but narrow forehead, the dark, voluptuous, but crafty and sinister eye, the features of the descendant of Charles V. It was the Infant of Spain that stood in the chamber of his ambitious minion.

"This is convenient, this private entrance into thy penetralia, Roderigo. It shelters me from the prying eyes of Uzeda, who ever seeks to cozen the sire by spying on the son. We will pay him off one of these days. He loves you no less than he does his prince."

"I bear no malice to him for that, your highness. He covets the smiles of the rising sun, and rails at the humble object which, he thinks, obstructs the beam."

"He might be easy on that score: I hate the man, and his cold formalities. He is ever fancying that we princes are intent on the affairs of State, and forgets that we are mortal, and that youth is the age for the bower, not the council. My precious Calderon, life would be dull without thee: how I rejoice at thy return, thou best inventor of pleasure that satiety ever prayed for! Nay, blush not: some men despise thee for thy talents; I do thee homage. By my great grandsire's beard, it will be a merry time at court when I am monarch, and thou minister!"

Calderon looked earnestly at the prince, but his scrutiny

did not serve to dispel a certain suspicion of the royal sincerity that ever and anon came across the favourite's most
sanguine dreams.   With all Philip's gayety, there was something restrained and latent in his ambiguous smile and his
calm, deep, brilliant eye.   Calderon, immeasurably above his
lord in genius, was scarcely, perhaps, the equal of that beard-
less boy in hypocrisy and craft, in selfish coldness, in matured
depravity.

"Well," resumed the prince, "I pay you not these compliments without an object.   I have need of you, — great need;
never did I so require your services as at this moment; never
was there so great demand on your invention, your courage,
your skill.   Know, Calderon, I love!"

"My prince," said the marquis, smiling, "it is certainly
not first love.   How often has your highness — "

"No," interrupted the prince, hastily, — "no, I never loved
till now.   We never can love what we can easily win; but
this, Calderon, *this* heart would be a conquest.   Listen.   I
was at the convent chapel of St. Mary of the White Sword
yesterday with the queen.   Thou knowest that the abbess
once was a lady of the chamber, and the queen loves her.
Both of us were moved and astonished by the voice of one of
the choir, — it was that of a novice.   After the ceremony the
queen made inquiries touching this new Santa Cecilia; and
who dost thou think she is?   No; thou wilt never guess! the
once celebrated singer, the beautiful, the inimitable Beatriz
Coello!   Ah, you may well look surprised; when actresses
turn nuns, it is well-nigh time for Calderon and Philip to
turn monks.   Now, you must know, Roderigo, that I, un-
worthy though I be, am the cause of this conversion.   There
is a certain Martin Fonseca, a kinsman of Lerma's — thou
knowest him well.   I learned, some time since, from the
duke, that this young Orlando was most madly enamoured of
a low-born girl, — nay, desired to wed her.   The duke's story
moved my curiosity.   I found that it was the young Beatriz
Coello, whom I had already admired on the stage.   Ah, Calderon, she blazed and set during thy dull mission to Lisbon!
I sought an opportunity to visit her.   I was astonished at her

beauty, that seemed more dazzling in the chamber than on the stage. I pressed my suit — in vain. Calderon, hear you that? — in vain! Why wert thou not by? Thy arts never fail, my friend! She was living with an old relation, or *gouvernante*. The old relation died suddenly; I took advantage of her loneliness; I entered her house at night. By Saint Jago, her virtue baffled and defeated me. The next morning she was gone; nor could my researches discover her, until, at the convent of St. Mary, I recognized the lost actress in the young novice. She has fled to the convent to be true to Fonseca; she must fly from the convent to bless the prince. This is my tale: I want thy aid."

"Prince," said Calderon, gravely, "thou knowest the laws of Spain, the rigour of the Church. I dare not — "

"Pshaw. No scruples — my rank will bear thee harmless. Nay, look not so demure; why, even thou, see, hast thy Armida. This billet in a female hand — Heaven and earth, Calderon! What name is this? Beatriz Coello! Darest thou have crossed my path? Speak, sir! — speak!"

"Your highness," said Calderon, with a mixture of respect and dignity in his manner, — "your highness, hear me. My first benefactor, my beloved pupil, my earliest patron, was the same Don Martin Fonseca who seeks this girl with an honest love. This morning he has visited me, to implore my intercession on his behalf. Oh, Prince! turn not away; thou knowest not half his merit. Thou knowest not the value of such subjects, — men of the old iron race of Spain. Thou hast a noble and royal heart; be not the rival to the defender of thy crown. Bless this brave soldier, spare this poor orphan, — and one generous act of self-denial shall give thee absolution for a thousand pleasures."

"This from Roderigo Calderon!" said the prince, with a bitter sneer. "Man, know thy station and thy profession. When I want homilies, I seek my confessor; when I have resolved on a vice, I come to thee. A truce with this bombast. For Fonseca, he shall be consoled; and when he shall learn who is his rival, he is a traitor if he remain discontented with his lot. Thou shalt aid me, Calderon!"

"Your highness will pardon me — no!"

"Do I hear right? No! Art thou not my minion, my instrument? Can I not destroy as I have helped to raise thee? Thy fortunes have turned thy brain. The king already suspects and dislikes thee; thy foe, Uzeda, has his ear. The people execrate thee. If I abandon thee, thou art lost. Look to it!"

Calderon remained mute and erect, with his arms folded on his breast, and his cheek flushed with suppressed passions. Philip gazed at him earnestly, and then, muttering to himself, approached the favourite with an altered air.

"Come, Calderon, I have been hasty, — you maddened me; I meant not to wound you. Thou art honest, I think thou lovest me; and I will own that in ordinary circumstances thy advice would be good, and thy scruples laudable. But I tell thee that I adore this girl; that I have set all my hopes upon her; that at whatever cost, whatever risk, she must be mine. Wilt *thou* desert me? Wilt thou, on whose faith I have ever leaned so trustingly, forsake thy friend and thy prince for this brawling soldier? No; I wrong thee."

"Oh," said Calderon, with much semblance of emotion, "I would lay down my life in your service, and I have often surrendered my conscience to your lightest will! But this would be so base a perfidy in me! He has confided his life to my hands. How canst even thou count on my faith, if thou knowest me false to another?"

"False! art thou not false to me? Have I not confided to thee, and dost thou not desert me, — nay, perhaps, betray? How wouldst thou serve this Fonseca? How liberate the novice?"

"By an order of the court. Your royal mother — "

"Enough!" said the prince, fiercely; "do so. Thou shalt have leisure for repentance."

As he spoke, Philip strode to the door. Calderon, alarmed and anxious, sought to detain him; but the prince broke disdainfully away and Calderon was again alone.

CHAPTER IV.

CIVIL AMBITION AND ECCLESIASTICAL.

SCARCELY had the prince vanished, before the door that led from the anteroom was opened, and an old man, in the ecclesiastical garb, entered the secretary's cabinet.

"Do I intrude, my son?" said the churchman.

"No, father, no; I never more desired your presence, your counsel. It is not often that I stand halting and irresolute between the two magnets of interest and conscience: this is one of those rare dilemmas."

Here Calderon rapidly narrated the substance of his conversation with Fonseca, and of the subsequent communication with the prince.

"You see," he said in conclusion, "how critical is my position. On one side, my obligations to Fonseca, my promise to a benefactor, a friend,— to the boy I assisted to rear. Nor is that all: the prince asks me to connive at the abstraction of a novice from a consecrated house. What peril! what hazard! On the other side, if I refuse, the displeasure, the vengeance of the prince, for whose favour I have already half forfeited that of the king; and who, were he once to frown upon me, would encourage all my enemies — in other phrase, the whole court — in one united attempt at my ruin."

"It is a stern trial," said the monk, gravely; "and one that may well excite your fear."

"Fear, Aliaga! — ha! ha! fear!" said Calderon, laughing scornfully. "Did true ambition ever know fear? Have we not the old Castilian proverb that tells us, 'He who has climbed the first step to power has left terror a thousand leagues behind'? No, it is not fear that renders me irresolute; it is wisdom, and some touch, some remnant, of human nature, — philosophers would call it virtue; you priests, religion."

"Son," said the priest, "when, as one of that sublime calling which enables us to place our unshodden feet upon the
necks of kings, I felt that I had the power to serve and to
exalt you; when, as confessor to Philip, I backed the patronage of Lerma, recommended you to the royal notice, and
brought you into the sunshine of the royal favour, it was because I had read in your heart and brain those qualities of
which the spiritual masters of the world ever seek to avail
their cause. I knew thee brave, crafty, aspiring, unscrupulous. I knew that thou wouldest not shrink at the means
that could secure to thee a noble end. Yea, when, years ago,
in the valley of the Xenil, I saw thee bathe thy hands in the
blood of thy foe, and heard thy laugh of exulting scorn; when
I, alone master of thy secret, beheld thee afterwards flying
from thy home stained with a second murder, but still calm,
stern, and lord of thine own reason, — my knowledge of mankind told me, 'Of such men are high converts and mighty in-
struments made!'"

The priest paused; for Calderon heard him not. His cheek
was livid, his eyes closed, his chest heaved wildly.

"Horrible remembrance!" he muttered; "fatal love! dread
revenge! Inez, Inez, what hast thou to answer for!"

"Be soothed, my son; I meant not to tear the bandage from
thy wounds."

"Who speaks?" cried Calderon, starting. "Ha, priest!
priest! I thought I heard the Dead. Talk on, talk on: talk
of the world, the Inquisition, thy plots, the torture, the rack!
Talk of aught that will lead me back from the past."

"No; let me for a moment lead thee thither, in order to
portray the future that awaits thee. When, at night, I found
thee — the blood-stained fugitive — cowering beneath the
shadow of the forest, dost thou remember that I laid my
hand upon thine arm, and said to thee, 'Thy life is in my
power'? From that hour, thy disdain of my threats, of
myself, of thine own life, — all made me view thee as one
born to advance our immortal cause. I led thee to safety far
away; I won thy friendship and thy confidence. Thou be-
camest one of us, — one of the great Order of Jesus. Subse-

quently, I placed thee as the tutor to young Fonseca, then heir to great fortunes. The second marriage of his uncle, and the heir that by that marriage interposed between him and the honour of his house, rendered the probable alliance of the youth profitless to us. But thou hadst procured his friendship. He presented thee to the Duke of Lerma. I was just then appointed confessor to the king; I found that years had ripened thy genius, and memory had blunted in thee all the affections of the flesh. Above all, hating, as thou didst, the very name of the Moor, thou wert the man of men to aid in our great design of expelling the accursed race from the land of Spain. Enough — I served thee, and thou didst repay us. Thou hast washed out thy crime in the blood of the infidel, — thou art safe from detection. In Roderigo Calderon, Marquis de Siete Iglesias, who will suspect the Roderigo Nunez, the murderous student of Salamanca? Our device of the false father stifled even curiosity. Thou mayest wake to the future, nor tremble at one shadow in the past. The brightest hopes are before us both; but to realize them, we must continue the same path. We must never halt at an obstacle in our way. We must hold that to be no crime which advances our common objects. Mesh upon mesh we must entangle the future monarch in our web, — thou, by the nets of pleasure; I, by those of superstition. The day that sees Philip the Fourth upon the throne must be a day of jubilee for the Brotherhood and the Inquisition. When thou art prime minister, and I grand inquisitor, — that time must come, — we shall have the power to extend the sway of the sect of Loyola to the ends of the Christian world. The Inquisition itself our tool, posterity shall regard us as the apostles of intellectual faith. And thinkest thou that, for the attainment of these great ends, we can have the tender scruples of common men? Perish a thousand Fonsecas, ten thousand novices, ere thou lose, by the strength of a hair, thy hold over the senses and soul of the licentious Philip! At whatever hazard, save thy power; for with it are bound, as mariners to a plank, the hopes of those who make the mind a sceptre."

"Thy enthusiasm blinds and misleads thee, Aliaga," said

Calderon, coldly. "For me, I tell thee now, as I have told thee before, that I care not a rush for thy grand objects. Let mankind serve itself,— I look to myself alone. But fear not my faith; my interests and my very life are identified with thee and thy fellow-fanatics. If I desert thee, thou art too deep in my secrets not to undo me; and were I to slay thee, in order to silence thy testimony, I know enough of thy fraternity to know that I should but raise up a multitude of avengers. As for this matter, you give me wise, if not pious counsel. I will consider well of it. Adieu! The hour summons me to attend the king."

CHAPTER V.

THE TRUE FATA MORGANA.

In the royal chamber, before a table covered with papers, sat the king and his secretary. Grave, sullen, and taciturn, there was little in the habitual manner of Philip the Third that could betray to the most experienced courtier the outward symptoms of favour or caprice. Education had fitted him for the cloister, but the necessities of despotism had added acute cunning to slavish superstition. The business for which Calderon had been summoned was despatched, with a silence broken but by monosyllables from the king, and brief explanations from the secretary; and Philip, rising, gave the signal for Calderon to retire. It was then that the king, turning a dull but steadfast eye upon the marquis, said, with a kind of effort, as if speech were painful to him,—

"The prince left me but a minute before your entrance; have you seen him since your return?"

"Your majesty, yes. He honoured me this morning with his presence."

"On State affairs?"

"Your majesty knows, I trust, that your servant treats of State affairs only with your august self, or your appointed ministers."

"The prince has favoured you, Don Roderigo."

"Your majesty commanded me to seek that favour."

"It is true. Happy the monarch whose faithful servant is the confidant of the heir to his crown!"

"Could the prince harbour one thought displeasing to your majesty, I think I could detect and quell it at its birth. But your majesty is blessed in a grateful son."

"I believe it. His love of pleasure decoys him from ambition — so it should be. I am not an austere parent. Keep his favour, Don Roderigo; it pleases me. Hast thou offended him in aught?"

"I trust I have not incurred so great a misfortune."

"He spoke not of thee with his usual praises — I noticed it. I tell thee this that thou mayest rectify what is wrong. Thou canst not serve me more than by guarding him from all friendships save with those whose affection to myself I can trust. I have said enough."

"Such has ever been my object. But I have not the youth of the prince, and men speak ill of me, that, in order to gain his confidence, I share in his pursuits."

"It matters not what they say of thee. Faithful ministers are rarely eulogized by the populace or the court. Thou knowest my mind: I repeat, lose not the prince's favour."

Calderon bowed low, and withdrew. As he passed through the apartments of the palace, he crossed a gallery, in which he perceived, stationed by a window, the young prince and his own arch-foe, the Duke d'Uzeda. At the same instant, from an opposite door, entered the Cardinal-Duke de Lerma; and the same unwelcome conjunction of hostile planets smote the eyes of that intriguing minister. Precisely because Uzeda was the duke's son was he the man in the world whom the duke most dreaded and suspected.

Whoever is acquainted with the Spanish comedy will not fail to have remarked the prodigality of intrigue and counter-intrigue upon which its interest is made to depend. In this, the Spanish comedy was the faithful mirror of the Spanish life, especially in the circles of a court. Men lived in a perfect labyrinth of plot and counter-plot. The spirit of *finesse,* manœuvre, subtlety, and double-dealing pervaded every family. Not a house that was not divided against itself !

As Lerma turned his eyes from the unwelcome spectacle of such sudden familiarity between Uzeda and the heir-apparent, — a familiarity which it had been his chief care to guard against, — his glance fell on Calderon. He beckoned to him in silence, and retired, unobserved by the two confabulators, through the same door by which he had entered. Calderon took the hint, and followed him. The duke entered a small room, and carefully closed the door.

"How is this, Calderon? " he asked, but in a timid tone, for the weak old man stood in awe of his favourite. "Whence this new and most ill-boding league? "

"I know not, your eminence; remember that I am but just returned to Madrid: it amazes me no less than it does your eminence."

"Learn the cause of it, my good Calderon: the prince ever professed to hate Uzeda. Restore him to those feelings: thou art all in all with his highness! If Uzeda once gain his ear, thou art lost."

"Not so," cried Calderon, proudly. "My service is to the king; I have a right to his royal protection, for I have a claim on his royal gratitude."

"Do not deceive thyself," said the duke, in a whisper: "The king cannot live long: I have it from the best authority, his physician; nor is this all, — a formidable conspiracy against thee exists at court. But for myself and the king's confessor, Philip would consent to thy ruin. The strong hold thou hast over him is in thy influence with the Infant, — an influence which he knows to be exerted on behalf of his own fearful and jealous policy; that influence gone, neither I nor Aliaga could suffice to protect thee. Enough! Shut every access to Philip's heart against Uzeda."

Calderon bowed in silence, and the duke hastened to the royal cabinet.

"What a fool was I to think that I could still wear a con·science!" muttered Calderon, with a sneering lip; "but, Uzeda, I will baffle thee yet."

The next morning, the Marquis de Siete Iglesias presented himself at the levee of the prince of Spain.

Around the favourite, as his proud stature towered above the rest, flocked the obsequious grandees. The haughty smile was yet on his lip when the door opened and the prince entered. The crowd, in parting suddenly, left Calderon immediately in front of Philip; who, after gazing on him sternly for a moment, turned away, with marked discourtesy, from the favourite's profound reverence, and began a low and smiling conversation with Gonsalez de Leon, one of Calderon's open foes.

The crowd exchanged looks of delight and surprise; and each of the nobles, before so wooing in their civilities to the minister, edged cautiously away.

His mortification had but begun. Presently Uzeda, hitherto almost a stranger to those apartments, appeared; the prince hastened to him, and in a few minutes the duke was seen following the prince into his private chamber. The sun of Calderon's favour seemed set. So thought the courtiers; not so the haughty favourite. There was even a smile of triumph on his lip, a sanguine flush upon his pale cheek, as he turned unheeding from the throng, and then entering his carriage, regained his home.

He had scarcely re-entered his cabinet, ere, faithful to his appointment, Fonseca was announced.

"What tidings, my best of friends?" exclaimed the soldier.

Calderon shook his head mournfully.

"My dear pupil," said he, in accents of well-affected sympathy, "there is no hope for thee. Forget this vain dream, —return to the army. I can promise thee promotion, rank, honours; but the hand of Beatriz is beyond my power."

"How?" said Fonseca, turning pale and sinking into a seat. "How is this? Why so sudden a change? Has the queen —"

"I have not seen her majesty; but the king is resolved

upon this matter: so are the Inquisition. The Church complains of recent and numerous examples of unholy and impolitic relaxation of her dread power. The court dare not interfere. The novice must be left to her own choice."

"And is there no hope?"

"None! Return to the excitement of thy brave career."

"Never!" cried Fonseca, with great vehemence. "If, in requital of all my services, of life risked, blood spilled, I cannot obtain a boon so easy to accord me, I renounce a service in which even fame has lost its charm. And hark you, Calderon, I tell you that I will *not* forego this pursuit. So fair, so innocent a victim shall not be condemned to that living tomb. Through the walls of the nunnery, through the spies of the Inquisition, love will find out its way; and in some distant land I will yet unite happiness and honour. I fear not exile; I fear not reverse; I no longer fear poverty itself. All lands, where the sound of the trumpet is not unknown, can afford career to the soldier, who asks from Heaven no other boon but his mistress and his sword."

"You will seek to abstract Beatriz, then?" said Calderon, calmly and musingly. "Yes, it may be your best course, if you take the requisite precautions. But can you see her; can you concert with her?"

"I think so. I trust I have already paved the way to an interview. Yesterday, after I quitted thee, I sought the convent; and as the chapel is one of the public sights of the city, I made my curiosity my excuse. Happily, I recognized in the porter of the convent an old servitor of my father's; he had known me from a child; he dislikes his calling, he will consent to accompany our flight, to share our fortunes; he has promised to convey a letter from me to Beatriz, and to transmit to me her answer."

"The stars smile on thee, Don Martin. When thou hast learned more, consult with me again *Now*, I see a way to assist thee."

CHAPTER VI.

WEB UPON WEB.

THE next day, to the discomfiture of the courtiers, Calderon and the Infant of Spain were seen together, publicly, on the parade; and the secretary made one of the favoured few who attended the prince at the theatre. His favour was greater, his power more dazzling, than ever it had been known before. No cause for the breach and reconciliation being known, some attributed it to caprice, others to the wily design of the astute Calderon for the humiliation of Uzeda, who seemed only to have been admitted to one smile from the rising sun in order more signally to be reconsigned to the shade.

Meanwhile, Fonseca prospered almost beyond his hopes. Young, ardent, sanguine, the poor novice had fled from her quiet home and the indulgence of her free thoughts to the chill solitude of the cloister, little dreaming of the extent of the change. With a heart that overflowed with the warm thoughts of love and youth, the ghostlike shapes that flitted round her, the icy forms, the rigid ceremonials of that life which is but the mimicry of death, appalled and shocked her. That she had preserved against a royal and most perilous, because unscrupulous suitor, her fidelity to the absent Fonseca, was her sole consolation.

Another circumstance had combined with the loss of her protectress and the absence of Don Martin to sadden her heart and dispose her to the cloister. On the deathbed of the old woman, who had been to her as a mother, she had learned a secret hitherto concealed from her tender youth. Dark and tragic were the influences of the star which had shone upon her birth, gloomy the heritage of memories associated with her parentage. A letter, of which she now became the guardian and treasurer,— a letter in her mother's hand, woke tears more deep and bitter than she had ever shed for herself. In that letter she read the strength and the fidelity, the sorrow and the gloom, of woman's love; and a dreary foreboding told her that the shadow of the mother's fate was cast over the child's. Such were the thoughts that made the cloister welcome till the desolation of the shelter was tried and known. But when, through the agency of the porter, Fonseca's letter reached her, all other feelings gave way to the burst of natural and passionate emotion. The absent had returned, again wooed, was still faithful. The awful vow was not spoken, — she might yet be his. She answered; she chided; she spoke of doubt, of peril, of fear for him, of maiden shame; but her affection coloured every word, and the letter was full of hope. The correspondence continued; the energetic remonstrances of Fonseca, the pure and fervent attachment of the novice, led more and more rapidly and surely to the inevitable result. Beatriz yielded to the prayer of her lover; she consented to the scheme of escape and flight that he proposed.

Late at evening Fonseca sought Calderon. The marquis was in the gardens of his splendid mansion.

The moonlight streamed over many a row of orange-trees and pomegranates, many a white and richly sculptured vase on its marble pedestal, many a fountain, that scattered its low music round the breathless air. Upon a terrace that commanded a stately view of the spires and palaces of Madrid stood Calderon, alone; beside him, one solitary and gigantic aloe cast its deep gloom of shade; and his motionless attitude, his folded arms, his face partially lifted to the starlit heavens, bespoke the earnestness and concentration of his thoughts.

"Why does this shudder come over me?" said he, half aloud. "It was thus in that dismal hour which preceded the knowledge of my shame, — the deed of a dark revenge, the revolution of my eventful and wondrous life! Ah, how happy was I once! a contented and tranquil student; a believer in those eyes that were to me as the stars to the astrologer. But the golden age passed into that of iron. And now," added Calderon, with a self-mocking sneer, "comes the era which the poets have not chronicled; for fraud and hypocrisy and vice know no poets!"

The quick step of Fonseca interrupted the courtier's revery. He turned, knit his brow, and sighed heavily, as if nerving himself to some effort; but his brow was smooth, and his aspect cheerful, ere Fonseca reached his side.

"Give me joy, give me joy, dear Calderon! She has consented. Now, then, your promised aid."

"You can depend upon the fidelity of your friendly porter?"

"With my life."

"A master key to the back-door of the chapel has been made?"

"See, I have it."

"And Beatriz can contrive to secrete herself in the confessional at the hour of the night prayers?"

"There is no doubt of her doing so with safety. The number of the novices is so great that one of them cannot well be missed."

"So much, then, for your part of the enterprise. Now for mine. You know that solitary house in the suburbs, on the high road to Fuencarral, which I pointed out to you yesterday? Well, the owner is a creature of mine. There horses shall be in waiting; there disguises shall be prepared. Beatriz must necessarily divest herself of the professional dress; you had better choose meaner garments for yourself. Drop those hidalgo titles of which your father is so proud, and pass off yourself and the novice as a notary and his wife, about to visit France on a lawsuit of inheritance. One of my secretaries shall provide you with a pass. Meanwhile, to-morrow, I shall be the first officially to hear of the flight of the novice, and I will set the pursuers on a wrong scent. Have I not arranged all things properly, my Fonseca?"

"You are our guardian angel!" cried Don Martin, fervently. "The prayers of Beatriz will be registered in your behalf above,— prayers that will reach the Great Throne as easily from the open valleys of France as in the gloomy cloisters of Madrid. At midnight to-morrow, then, we seek the house you have described to us."

"Ay, at midnight all shall be prepared."

With a light step and exulting heart, Fonseca turned from the palace of Calderon. Naturally sanguine and high-spirited, visions of hope and joy floated before his eyes, and the future seemed to him a land owning but the twin deities of Glory and Love.

He had reached about the centre of the street in which Calderon's abode was placed, when six men, who for some moments had been watching him from a little distance, approached.

"I believe," said the one who appeared the chief of the band, "that I have the honour to address Señor Don Martin Fonseca?"

"Such is my name."

"In the name of the king we arrest you. Follow us."

"Arrest! on what plea? What is my offence?"

"It is stated on this writ, signed by his Eminence the Cardinal-Duke de Lerma. You are charged with the crime of desertion."

"Thou liest, knave! I had the general's free permission to quit the camp."

"We have said all,— follow!"

Fonseca, naturally of the most impetuous and passionate character, was not in that moment in a mood to calculate coldly all the consequences of resistance. Arrest, imprisonment, on the eve before that which was to see him the deliverer of Beatriz, constituted a sentence of such despair, that all other considerations vanished before it. He set his teeth firmly, drew his sword, dashed aside the alguazil who attempted to obstruct his path, and strode grimly on, shaking one clenched hand in defiance, while with the other he waved the good Toledo that had often blazed in the van of battle, at the war-cry of "Saint Iago and Spain!"

The alguazils closed round the soldier, and the clash of swords was already heard, when suddenly torches borne on high threw their glare across the moonlit street, and two running footmen called out, "Make way for the most noble the Marquis de Siete Iglesias!" At that name, Fonseca dropped the point of his weapon; the alguazils themselves drew aside; and the tall figure and pale countenance of Calderon were visible amongst the group.

"What means this brawl in the open streets at this late hour?" said the minister, sternly.

"Calderon!" exclaimed Fonseca; "this is indeed fortunate! These caitiffs have dared to lay hands on a soldier of Spain, and to forge for their villany the name of his own kinsman, the Duke de Lerma."

"Your charge against this gentleman?" asked Calderon, calmly, turning to the principal alguazil, who placed the writ of arrest in the secretary's hand. Calderon read it leisurely, and raised his hat as he returned it to the alguazil; he then drew aside Fonseca.

"Are you mad?" said he, in a whisper. "Do you think you can resist the law? Had I not arrived so opportunely you would have converted a slight accusation into a capital offence. Go with these men: do not fear; I will see the duke, and obtain your immediate release. To-morrow I will visit and accompany you home."

Fonseca, still half beside himself with rage, would have replied, but Calderon significantly placed his finger on his lip, and turned to the alguazils.

"There is a mistake here: it will be rectified to-morrow. Treat this cavalier with all the respect and worship due to his birth and merits. Go, Don Martin, go," he added, in a lower voice; "go, unless you desire to lose Beatriz forever. Nothing but obedience can save you from the imprisonment of half a life!"

Awed and subdued by this threat, Fonseca, in gloomy silence, placed his sword in its sheath, and sullenly followed the alguazils. Calderon watched them depart with a thoughtful and absent look; then, starting from his revery, he bade his torchbearers proceed, and resumed his way to the Prince of Spain.

CHAPTER VII.

THE OPEN COUNTENANCE, THE CONCEALED THOUGHTS.

THE next day, at noon, Calderon visited Fonseca in his place of confinement. The young man was seated by a window that overlooked a large dull courtyard, with a neglected and broken fountain in the centre, leaning his cheek upon his hand. His long hair was dishevelled, his dress disordered, and a gloomy frown darkened features naturally open and ingenuous. He started to his feet as Calderon approached.

"My release — you have brought my release — let us forth!"

"My dear pupil, be ruled, be calm. I have seen the duke; the cause of your imprisonment is as I suspected. Some imprudent words, overheard, perhaps, but by your valet, have escaped you, — words intimating your resolution not to abandon Beatriz. You know your kinsman, a man of doubts and fears, of forms, ceremonies, and scruples. From very affection for his kindred and yourself he has contrived your arrest; all my expostulations have been in vain. I fear your imprisonment may continue, either until you give a solemn promise to renounce all endeavour to dissuade Beatriz from the final vows, or until she herself has pronounced them."

Fonseca, as if stupefied, stared a moment at Calderon, and then burst into a wild laugh. Calderon continued, —

"Nevertheless, do not despair. Be patient; I am ever about the duke; nay, I have the courage, in your cause, to appeal even to the king himself."

"And to-night she expects me, — to-night she was to be free!"

"We can convey the intelligence of your mischance to her: the porter will befriend you."

"Away, false friend, or powerless protector, that you are! Are your promises of aid come to this? But I care not; my case, my wrongs, shall be laid before the king; I will inquire if it be thus that Philip the Third treats the defenders of his crown.   Don Roderigo Calderon, will you place my memorial in the hands of your royal master?   Do this, and I will thank you."

"No, Fonseca, I will not ruin you; the king would pass your memorial to the Duke de Lerma.   Tush! this is not the way that men of sense deal with misfortune.   Think you I should be what I now am, if in every reverse I had raved, and not reflected?   Sit down, and let us think of what can now be done."

"Nothing, unless the prison door open by sunset."

"Stay, a thought strikes me.   The term of your imprisonment ceases when you relinquish the hope of Beatriz.   But what if the duke could believe that Beatriz relinquished *you?* What, for instance, if she fled from the convent as you proposed, and we could persuade the duke that it was with another?"

"Ah, be silent!"

"Nay, what advantages in this scheme! what safety!   If she fly alone, or, as supposed, with another lover, the duke will have no interest in pursuit, in punishment.   She is not of that birth that the State will take the trouble very actively to interfere; she may reach France in safety,—ay, a thousand times more safely than if she fled with you, a hidalgo and a man of rank, whom the State would have an interest to reclaim, and to whom the Inquisition, hating the nobles, would impute the crime of sacrilege.   It is an excellent thought!   Your imprisonment may be the salvation of you both; your plan may succeed still better without your intervention; and after a few days, the duke, believing that your resentment must necessarily replace your love, will order your release; you can join Beatriz on the frontier, and escape with her to France."

"But," said Fonseca, struck, but not convinced, by the suggestion of Calderon, "who will take my place with Beatriz; who penetrate into the gardens; who bear her from the convent?"

"That, for your sake, will I do. Perhaps," added Calderon, smiling, "a courtier may manage such an intrigue with even more dexterity than a soldier. I will bear her to the house we spoke of; there I know she can lie hid in safety, till the languid pursuit of uninterested officials shall cease; and thence I can easily find means to transport her, under safe and honourable escort, to any place it may please you to appoint."

"And think you Beatriz will fly with you, a stranger? Impossible! Your plan pleases me not."

"Nor does it please me," said Calderon, coldly; "the risks I proposed to run are too imminent to be contemplated complacently: I thank you for releasing me from my offer; nor should I have made it, Fonseca, but from this fear, — what if to-morrow the duke himself (he is a churchman, remember) see the novice; what if he terrify her with threats against yourself; what if he induce the abbess and the Church to abridge the novitiate; what if Beatriz be compelled or awed into taking the veil; what if you be released even next week and find her lost to you forever?"

"They cannot, — they dare not!"

"The duke dares all things for ambition; your alliance with Beatriz he would hold a disgrace to his house. Think not my warnings are without foundation, — I speak from authority; such is the course the Duke de Lerma *has* resolved upon. Nothing else could have induced me to offer to brave for your sake all the hazard of outraging the law and braving the terrors of the Inquisition. But let us think of some other plan. Is your escape possible? I fear not. No; you must trust to my chance of persuading the duke into prosecuting the matter no further; trust to some mightier scheme engrossing all his thoughts, — to a fit of good-humour after his siesta, or perhaps an attack of the gout or a stroke of apoplexy. Such, after all, are the chances of human felicity, the pivots on which turns the solemn wheel of human life."

Fonseca made no reply for some moments; he traversed the room with hasty and disordered strides, and at last stopped abruptly.

"Calderon, there is no option; I must throw myself on your generosity, your faith, your friendship. I will write to Beatriz; I will tell her, for my sake, to confide in you."

As he spoke, Don Martin turned to the table, and wrote a hasty and impassioned note, in which he implored the novice to trust herself to the directions of Don Roderigo Calderon, his best, his only friend; and as he placed this letter in the hands of the courtier, he turned aside to conceal his emotions. Calderon himself was deeply moved: his cheek was flushed, and his hand seemed tremulous as it took the letter.

"Remember," said Fonseca, "that I trust to you my life of life. As you are true to me, may Heaven be merciful to you!"

Calderon made no answer, but turned to the door.

"Stay," said Fonseca; "I had forgot this,— here is the master key."

"True; how dull I was! And the porter — will he attend to thy proxy?"

"Doubt it not. Accost him with the word, 'Grenada.' But he expects to share the flight."

"That can be arranged. To-morrow you will hear of my success. Farewell!"

CHAPTER VIII.

THE ESCAPE.

IT was midnight in the chapel of the convent.

The moonlight shone with exceeding lustre through the tall casements, and lit into a ghastly semblance of life the marble images of saint and martyr, that threw their long shadows over the consecrated floor. Nothing could well be conceived more dreary, solemn, and sepulchral than that holy place: its distained and time-hallowed walls; the impenetrable mass of darkness that gathered into those recesses which the moonlight failed to reach; its antique and massive tombs, above which reclined the sculptured effigies of some departed patroness or abbess, who had exchanged a living grave for the Mansions of the Blest. But there — oh, wonderful human heart! — even there, in that spot, the very homily and warning against earthly affections and mortal hopes — even there, couldst thou beat with as wild, as bright, and as pure a passion as ever heaved the breast and shone in the eyes of Beauty, in the free air that ripples the Guadiana, or amidst the twilight dance of Castilian maids.

A tall figure, wrapped from head to foot in a cloak, passed slowly up the aisle; but light and cautious though the footstep, it woke a low, hollow, ominous echo, that seemed more than the step itself to disturb the sanctity of the place. It paused opposite to a confessional, which was but dimly visible through the shadows around it; and then there emerged timidly a female form; and a soft voice whispered, "It is thou, Fonseca?"

"Hist!" was the answer; "he waits without. Be quick; speak not, come."

Beatriz recoiled in surprise and alarm at the voice of a stranger; but the man, seizing her by the hand, drew her hastily from the chapel, and hurried her across the garden, through a small postern door, which stood ajar, into an obscure street bordering the convent wall. Here stood the expectant porter, with a bundle in his hand, which he opened, and took thence a long cloak, such as the women of middling rank in Madrid wore in the winter season, with the customary mantilla or veil. With these, still without speaking, the stranger hastily shrouded the form of the novice, and once more hurried her on till about a hundred yards from the garden gate he came to a carriage, into which he lifted Beatriz, whispered a few words to the porter, seated himself by the side of the novice, and the vehicle drove rapidly away.

It was some moments before Beatriz could sufficiently recover from her first agitation and terror, to feel alive to all the strangeness of her situation. She was alone with a stranger; where was Fonseca? She turned towards her companion.

"Who art thou?" she said; "whither art thou leading me, and why — "

"Why is not Don Martin by thy side? Pardon me, señora: I have a billet for thee from Fonseca; in a few minutes thou wilt know all."

At this time the vehicle came suddenly in the midst of a train of footmen and equipages that choked up the way. There was a brilliant entertainment at the French embassy, and thither flocked all the rank and chivalry of Madrid. Calderon drew down the blinds and hastily enjoined silence on Beatriz. It was some minutes before the driver extricated himself from the throng; and then, as if to make amends for the delay, he put his horses to their full speed, and carefully selected the most obscure and solitary thoroughfares. At length the carriage entered the range of suburbs which still at this day the traveller passes on his road from Madrid to France. The horses stopped before a lonely house that stood a little apart from the road, and which from the fashion of its architecture appeared of considerable antiquity. The stranger descended and knocked twice at the door; it was opened by an old man, whose exaggerated features, bended frame, and long beard proclaimed him of the race of Israel. After a short and whispered parley, the stranger returned to Beatriz, gravely assisted her from the carriage, and, leading her across the threshold and up a flight of rude stairs, dimly lighted, entered a chamber richly furnished. The walls were hung with stuffs of gorgeous colouring and elaborate design. Pedestals of the whitest marble placed at each corner of the room supported candelabra of silver. The sofas and couches were of the heavy but sumptuous fashion which then prevailed in the palaces of France and Spain; and of which Venice (the true model of the barbaric decorations with which Louis the Fourteenth corrupted the taste of Paris) was probably the original inventor. In an alcove, beneath a silken canopy, was prepared a table, laden with wines, fruits, and viands; and altogether the elegance and luxury that characterized the apartment were in strong and strange contrast with the half-ruined exterior of the abode, the gloomy and rude approach to the chamber, and the mean and servile aspect of the Jew, who stood, or rather cowered by the door, as if waiting for further orders. With a wave of the hand the stranger dismissed the Israelite; and then, approaching Beatriz, presented to her Fonseca's letter.

As with an enchanting mixture of modesty and eagerness Beatriz, half averting her face, bent over the well-known characters, Calderon gazed upon her with a scrutinizing and curious eye.

The courtier was not, in this instance, altogether the villain that from outward appearances the reader may have deemed him. His plan was this: he had resolved on compliance with the wishes of the prince — his safety rested on that compliance. But Fonseca was not to be sacrificed without reserve. Profoundly despising womankind, and firmly persuaded of their constitutional treachery and deceit, Calderon could not believe the actress that angel of light and purity which she seemed to the enamoured Fonseca. He had resolved to subject her to the ordeal of the prince's addresses. If she fell, should he not save his friend from being the dupe of an artful *intriguante ;* should he not deserve the thanks of Don Martin for the very temptation to which Beatriz was now to be submitted? If he could convince Fonseca of her falsehood, he should stand acquitted to his friend, while he should have secured his interest with the prince. But if, on the other hand, Beatriz came spotless through the trial; if the prince, stung by her obstinate virtue, should menace to sink courtship into violence, Calderon knew that it would not be in the first or second interview that the novice would have any real danger to apprehend; and he should have leisure to concert her escape by such means as would completely conceal from the prince his own connivance at her flight. Such was the compromise that Calderon had effected between his conscience and his ambition. But while he gazed upon the novice, though her features were turned from him, and half veiled by the head-dress she had assumed, strange feelings, ominous and startling, like those remembrances of the Past which sometimes come in the guise of prophecies of the Future,

thronged, indistinct and dim, upon his breast. The uncon-
scious and exquisite grace of her form, its touching youth, an
air of innocence diffused around it, a something helpless and
pleading to man's protection in the very slightness of her
beautiful but fairy-like proportions, seemed to reproach his
treachery, and to awaken whatever of pity or human softness
remained in his heart.

The novice had read the letter; and turning, in the impulse
of surprise and alarm, to Calderon for explanation, for the
first time she remarked his features and his aspect; for he
had then laid aside his cloak, and the broad Spanish hat with
its heavy plume. It was thus that their eyes met, and, as
they did so, Beatriz, starting from her seat, uttered a wild
cry.

"And thy name is Calderon,— Don Roderigo Calderon?
Is it possible? Hadst thou never another name?" she exclaimed; and, as she spoke, she approached him slowly and
fearfully.

"Lady, Calderon is my name," replied the marquis; but
his voice faltered. "But thine — thine — is it, in truth,
Beatriz Coello?"

Beatriz made no reply, but continued to advance, till her
very breath came upon his cheek; she then laid her hand
upon his arm, and looked up into his face with a gaze so
earnest, so intent, so prolonged, that Calderon, but for a
strange and terrible thought — half of wonder, half of suspicion, which had gradually crept into his soul, and now
usurped it — might have doubted whether the reason of the
poor novice was not unsettled.

Slowly Beatriz withdrew her eyes, and they fell upon a
large mirror opposite, which reflected in full light the features of Calderon and herself. It was then — her natural
bloom having faded into a paleness scarcely less statue-like
than that which characterized the cheek of Calderon himself,
and all the sweet play and mobility of feature that belong to
first youth being replaced by a rigid and marble stillness of
expression, — it was then that a remarkable resemblance between these two persons became visible and startling. That

resemblance struck alike, and in the same instant, both Beatriz and Calderon; and both, gazing on the mirror, uttered an involuntary and simultaneous exclamation.

With a trembling and hasty hand the novice searched amidst the folds of her robe, and drew forth a small leathern case closed with clasps of silver. She touched the spring, and took out a miniature, upon which she cast a rapid and wild glance; then, lifting her eyes to Calderon, she cried, "It must be so! it is, it is my father!" and fell motionless at his feet.

Calderon did not for some moments heed the condition of the novice: that chamber, the meditated victim, the present time, the coming evil,— all were swept away from his soul; he was transported back into the past, with the two dread Spirits, Memory and Conscience. His knees knocked together, his aspect was livid, the cold drops stood upon his brow; he muttered incoherently, and then bent down and took up the picture. It was the face of a man in the plain garb of a Salamanca student, and in the first flush of youth; the noble brow, serene and calm, and stamped alike with candour and courage; the smooth cheek, rich with the hues of health; the lips, parting in a happy smile, and eloquent of joy and hope,— it was the face of that wily, grasping, ambitious, unscrupulous man, when life had yet brought no sin; it was as if the ghost of youth were come back to accuse the crimes of manhood! The miniature fell from his hand; he groaned aloud. Then gazing on the prostrate form of the novice, he said, "Poor wretch! can I believe that thou art indeed of mine own race and blood; or rather, does not nature, that stamped these lineaments on thy countenance, deceive and mock me? If she, thy mother, lied, why not nature herself?"

He raised the novice in his arms, and gazed long and wistfully upon her lifeless but most lovely features. She moved not,— she scarcely seemed to breathe; yet he fancied he felt her embrace tightening round him, he fancied he heard again the voice that had hailed him "FATHER!" His heart beat aloud; the divine instinct overpowered all things, he pressed a passionate kiss upon her forehead, and his tears fell fast

and warm upon her cheek.   But again the dark remembrance
crossed him, and he shuddered, placed the novice hastily on
one of the couches, and shouted aloud.

The Jew appeared, and was ordered to summon Jacinta.
A young woman of the same persuasion, and of harsh and
forbidding exterior, entered, and to her care Calderon briefly
consigned the yet insensible Beatriz.

While Jacinta unlaced the dress and chafed the temples of
the novice, Calderon seemed buried in gloomy thought.   At
last he strode slowly away, as if to quit the chamber, when
his foot struck against the case of the picture, and his
eye rested upon a paper which lay therein, folded and em-
bedded.   He took it up, and, lifting aside the hangings, hurried into a small cabinet lighted by a single lamp.   Here,
alone and unseen, Calderon read the following letter: —

TO RODERIGO NUNEZ.

Will this letter ever meet thine eyes?   I know not; but it is comfort to write to thee on the bed of death; and were it not for that horrible and haunting thought that thou believest me — me, whose very life
was in thy love — faithless and dishonoured, even death itself would be
the sweeter because it comes from the loss of thee.   Yes, something
tells me that these lines will not be written in vain; that thou wilt read
them yet, when this hand is still and this brain at rest, and that then
thou wilt feel that I could not have dared to write to thee if I were not
innocent; that in every word thou wilt recognize the evidence that is
strong as the voice of thousands, — the simple but solemn evidence of
faith and truth.   What! when for thee I deserted all, — home, and a
father's love, wealth, and the name I had inherited from Moors who had
been monarchs in their day, — couldst thou think that I had not made
the love of thee the core and life and principle of my very being!   And
one short year — could that suffice to shake my faith? — one year of
marriage, but two months of absence?   You left me, left that dear
home, by the silver Xenil.   For love did not suffice to you; ambition
began to stir within you, and you called it "love."   You said, it
grieved you that I was poor; that you could not restore to me the
luxury and wealth I had lost.   Alas! why did you turn so incredulously
from my assurance that in you, and you alone, were centred my ambition and pride?   You declared that the vain readers of the stars had

foretold at your cradle that you were predestined to lofty honours and dazzling power, and that the prophecy would work out its own fulfilment. You left me to seek in Madrid your relation who had risen into the favour of a minister, and from whose love you expected to gain an opening to your career. Do you remember how we parted, — how you kissed away my tears, and how they gushed forth again; how again and again you said, "Farewell!" and again and again returned as if we could never part? And I took my babe, but a few weeks born, from her cradle, and placed her in thy arms, and bade thee see that she had already learned thy smile; and were these the signs of falsehood? Oh, how I pined for the sound of thy footstep when thou wert gone! how all the summer had vanished from the landscape; and how, turning to thy child, I fancied I again beheld thee! The day after thou hadst left me there was a knock at the door of the cottage; the nurse opened it, and there entered your former rival, whom my father had sought to force upon me, the richest of the descendants of the Moor, Arraez Ferrares. Why linger on this hateful subject? He had tracked us to our home, he had learned thy absence, he came to insult me with his vows. By the Blessed Mother, whom thou hast taught me to adore, by the terror and pang of death, by my hopes of heaven, I am innocent, Roderigo, I am innocent! Oh, how couldst thou be so deceived? He quitted the cottage, discomfited and enraged; again he sought me, and again and again; and when the door was closed upon him, he waylaid my steps. Lone and defenceless as we were, thy wife and child, with but one attendant, I feared him not; but I trembled at thy return, for I knew that thou wert a Spaniard, a Castilian, and that beneath thy calm and gentle seeming lurked pride and jealousy and revenge. Thy letter came, the only letter since thy absence, the last letter from thee I may ever weep over, and lay upon my heart. Thy relation was dead, and his wealth enriched a nearer heir. Thou wert to return. The day in which I might expect thee approached, — it arrived. During the last week I had seen and heard no more of Ferrares. I trusted that he had at length discovered the vanity of his pursuit. I walked into the valley, thy child in my arms, to meet thee; but thou didst not come. The sun set, and the light of thine eyes replaced not the declining day. I returned home, and watched for thee all night, but in vain. The next morning again I went forth into the valley, and again, with a sick heart, returned to my desolate home. It was then noon. As I approached the door I perceived Ferrares. He forced his entrance. I told him of thy expected return, and threatened him with thy resentment. He left me; and, terrified with a thousand vague forebodings, I sat down to weep. The nurse, Leonarda, was watching by the cradle of our child in the inner room. I was alone. Suddenly the door opened. I heard thy step; I knew it; I knew its music. I started up. Saints of Heaven! what a meeting! what a return! Pale, haggard, thine hands and garments dripping blood, thine eyes blazing with insane fire, a terrible smile of mockery on thy lip, thou stoodst before me. I would have thrown myself on thy breast; thou didst cast me from thee; I fell on my knees, and thy blade was pointed at my heart, — the heart so full of thee! "He is dead," didst thou say, in a hollow voice; "he is dead — thy paramour — take thy bed beside him!" I know not what I said, but it seemed to move thee; thy hand trembled, and the point of thy weapon dropped. It was then that, hearing thy voice, Leonarda hastened into the room, and bore in her arms thy child. "See," I exclaimed, "see thy daughter; see, she stretches her hands to thee, — she pleads for her mother!" At that sight thy brow became dark, the demon seized upon thee again. "Mine!" were thy cruel words — they ring in my ear still — "no! she was born before the time — ha! ha! — thou didst betray me from the first!" With that thou didst raise thy sword; but even then (ah, blessed thought! even then) remorse and love palsied thy hand, and averted thy gaze: the blow was not that of death. I fell senseless to the ground, and when I recovered thou wert gone. Delirium succeeded; and when once more my senses and reason returned to me, I found by my side a holy priest, and from him, gradually, I learned all that till then was dark. Ferrares had been found in the valley, weltering in his blood. Borne to a neighbouring monastery, he lingered a few days, to confess the treachery he had practised on thee; to adopt, in his last hours, the Christian faith; and to attest his crime with his own signature. He enjoined the monk, who had converted and confessed him, to place this proof of my innocence in my hands. Behold it enclosed within. If this letter ever reach thee, thou wilt learn how thy wife was true to thee in life, and has therefore the right to bless thee in death.

At this passage, Calderon dropped the letter, and was seized with a kind of paralysis, which for some moments seemed to deprive him of life itself. When he recovered he eagerly grasped a scroll that was inclosed in the letter, but which, hitherto, he had disregarded. Even then, so strong were his emotions, that sight itself was obscured and dimmed, and it was long before he could read the characters, which were already discoloured by time.

TO INEZ.

I have but a few hours to live, — let me spend them in atonement and in prayer, less for myself than thee. Thou knowest not how madly I adored thee; and how thy hatred or indifference stung every passion into torture. Let this pass. When I saw thee again, — the forsaker of thy faith, poor, obscure, and doomed to a peasant's lot, — daring hopes shaped themselves into fierce resolves. Finding that thou wert inexorable, I turned my arts upon thy husband. I knew his poverty and his ambition : we Moors have had ample knowledge of the avarice of the Christians ! I bade one whom I could trust to seek him out at Madrid. Wealth — lavish wealth — wealth that could open to a Spaniard all the gates of power was offered to him if he would renounce thee forever. Nay, in order to crush out all love from his breast, it was told him that mine was the prior right, — that thou hadst yielded to my suit ere thou didst fly with him ; that thou didst use his love as an escape from thine own dishonour; that thy very child owned another father. I had learned, and I availed myself of the knowledge, that it was born before its time. We had miscalculated the effect of this representation, backed and supported by forged letters ; instead of abandoning thee, he thought only of revenge for his shame. As I left thy house, the last time I gazed upon thine indignant eyes, I found the avenger on my path ! He had seen me quit thy roof, — he needed no other confirmation of the tale. I fell into the pit which I had digged for thee. Conscience unnerved my hand and blunted my sword ; our blades scarcely crossed before his weapon stretched me on the ground. They tell me he has fled from the anger of the law ; let him return without a fear. Solemnly, and from the bed of death, and in the sight of the last tribunal, I proclaim to justice and the world that we fought fairly, and I perish justly. I have adopted thy faith, though I cannot comprehend its mysteries. It is enough that it holds out to me the only hope that we shall meet again. I direct these lines to be transmitted to thee, — an eternal proof of thy innocence and my guilt. Ah, canst thou forgive me ? I knew no sin till I knew thee.

ARRAEZ FERRARES.

Calderon paused ere he turned to the concluding lines of his wife's letter; and, though he remained motionless and speechless, never wore agony and despair stamped more terribly on the face of man.

CONCLUSION OF THE LETTER OF INEZ.

And what avails to me this testimony of my faith ?　Thou art fled ; they cannot track thy footsteps ; I shall see thee no more on earth.　I am dying fast, but not of the wound I took from thee ; let not that thought darken thy soul, my husband !　No, that wound is healed. Thought is sharper than the sword.　I have pined away for the loss of thee and thy love !　Can the shadow live without the sun ?　And wilt thou never place thy hands on my daughter's head, and bless her for her mother's sake ?　Ah, yes, yes !　The saints that watch over our human destinies will one day cast her in thy way : and the same hour that gives thee a daughter shall redeem and hallow the memory of a wife. . . .　Leonarda has vowed to be a mother to our child ; to tend her, work for her, rear her, though in poverty, to virtue.　I consign these letters to Leonarda's charge, with thy picture, — never to be removed from my breast till the heart within has ceased to beat.　Not till Beatriz (I have so baptized her — it was thy mother's name !) has attained to the age when reason can wrestle with the knowledge of sorrow, shall her years be shadowed with the knowledge of our fate. Leonarda has persuaded me that Beatriz shall not take thy name of Nunez.　Our tale has excited horror — for it is not understood — and thou art called the murderer of thy wife ; and the story of our misfortunes would cling to our daughter's life, and reach her ears, and perhaps mar her fate.　But I know that thou wilt discover her not the less, for Nature has a Providence of its own.　When at last you meet her, protect, guard, love her, — sacred to you as she is, and shall be, the pure but mournful legacy of love and death.　I have done : I die blessing thee !

INEZ.

Scarce had he finished those last words, ere the clock struck : it was the hour in which the prince was to arrive. The thought restored Calderon to the sense of the present time, — the approaching peril.　All the cold calculations he had formed for the stranger-novice vanished now.　He kissed the letter passionately, placed it in his breast, and hurried into the chamber where he had left his child.　Our tale returns to Fonseca.

CHAPTER IX.

THE COUNTERPLOT.

CALDERON had not long left the young soldier before the governor of the prison entered to pay his respects to a captive of such high birth and military reputation.

Fonseca, always blunt and impatient of mood, was not in a humour to receive and return compliments; but the governor had scarcely seated himself ere he struck a chord in the conversation which immediately arrested the attention and engaged the interest of the prisoner.

"Do not fear, sir," said he, "that you will be long detained; the power of your enemy is great, but it will not be of duration. The storm is already gathering round him; he must be more than man if he escape the thunderbolt."

"Do you speak to me thus of my own kinsman, the Cardinal-Duke de Lerma?"

"No, Don Martin, pardon me. I spoke of the Marquis de Siete Iglesias. Are you so great a stranger to Madrid and to the court as to suppose that the Cardinal de Lerma ever signs a paper but at the instance of Don Roderigo? Nay, that he ever looks over the paper to which he sets his hand? Depend upon it, you are here to gratify the avarice or revenge of the Scourge of Spain."

"Impossible!" cried Fonseca. "Don Roderigo is my friend, my intercessor. He overwhelms me with his kindness."

"Then you are indeed lost," said the governor, in accents of compassion; "the tiger always caresses his prey before he devours it. What have you done to provoke his kindness?"

"Señor," said Fonseca, suspiciously, "you speak with a strange want of caution to a stranger, and against a man whose power you confess."

"Because I am safe from his revenge; because the Inquisition have already fixed their fatal eyes upon him; because by that Inquisition I am not unknown nor unprotected; because I see with joy and triumph the hour approaching that must render up to justice the pander of the prince, the betrayer of the king, the robber of the people; because I have an interest in thee, Don Martin, of which thou wilt be aware when thou hast learned my name. I am Juan de la Nuza, the father of the young officer whose life you saved in the assault of the Moriscos, in Valentia, and I owe you an everlasting gratitude."

There was something in the frank and hearty tone of the governor which at once won Fonseca's confidence. He became agitated and distracted with suspicions of his former tutor and present patron.

"What, I ask, hast thou done to attract his notice? Calderon is not capricious in cruelty. Art thou rich, and does he hope that thou wilt purchase freedom with five thousand pistoles? No! Hast thou crossed the path of his ambition? Hast thou been seen with Uzeda? Or art thou in favour with the prince? No, again! Then hast thou some wife, some sister, some mistress, of rare accomplishments and beauty, with whom Calderon would gorge the fancy and retain the esteem of the profligate Infant? Ah, thou changest colour."

"By Heaven! you madden me with these devilish surmises. Speak plainly."

"I see thou knowest not Calderon," said the governor, with a bitter smile. "I do,— for my niece was beautiful, and the prince wooed her — But enough of that: at his scaffold, or at the rack, I shall be avenged on Roderigo Calderon. You said the cardinal was your kinsman; you are, then, equally related to his son, the Duke d'Uzeda. Apply not to Lerma; he is the tool of Calderon. Apply yourself to Uzeda; he is Calderon's mortal foe. While Calderon gains ground with the prince, Uzeda advances with the king. Uzeda by a word can procure thy release. The duke knows and trusts me. Shall I be commissioned to acquaint him with thy arrest, and entreat his intercession with Philip?"

"You give me new life! But not an hour is to be lost; this night — this day — oh, Mother of Mercy! what image have you conjured up! fly to Uzeda, if you would save my very reason. I myself have scarcely seen him since my boyhood, — Lerma forbade me seek his friendship. But I am of his race, — his blood."

"Be cheered, — I shall see the duke to-day. I have business with him where you wot not. We are bringing strange events to a crisis. Hope the best."

With this the governor took his leave.

At the dusk of the evening, Don Juan de la Nuza, wrapped in a dark mantle, stood before a small door deep-set in a massive and gloomy wall, that stretched along one side of a shunned and deserted street. Without sign of living hand the door opened at his knock, and the governor entered a long and narrow passage that conducted to chambers more associated with images of awe than any in his own prison. Here he suddenly encountered the Jesuit, Fray Louis d'Aliaga, confessor to the king.

"How fares the Grand Inquisitor?" asked De la Nuza.

"He has just breathed his last," answered the Jesuit. "His illness — so sudden — defied all aid. Sandoval y Roxas is with the saints."

The governor, who was, as the reader may suppose, one of the sacred body, crossed himself, and answered: "With whom will rest the appointment of the successor? Who will be first to gain the ear of the king?"

"I know not," replied the Jesuit; "but I am at this instant summoned to Uzeda. Pardon my haste."

So saying, Aliaga glided away

"With Sandoval y Roxas," muttered Don Juan, "dies the last protector of Calderon and Lerma: unless, indeed, the wily marquis can persuade the king to make Aliaga, his friend, the late cardinal's successor. But Aliaga seeks Uzeda, — Uzeda his foe and rival. What can this portend?"

Thus soliloquizing, the governor silently continued his way till he came to a door by which stood two men, masked, who saluted him with a mute inclination of the head. The door opened and again closed, as the governor entered.

Meanwhile, the confessor had gained the palace of the Duke d'Uzeda. Uzeda was not alone: with him was a man whose sallow complexion, ill-favoured features, and simple dress strangely contrasted the showy person and sumptuous habiliments of the duke. But the instant this personage opened his lips the comparison was no longer to his prejudice. Something in the sparkle of his deep-set eye, in the singular enchantment of his smile, and above all, in the tone of a very musical and earnest voice, chained attention at once to his words. And, whatever those words, there was about the man, and his mode of thought and expression, the stamp of a mind at once crafty and commanding. This personage was Gaspar de Guzman, then but a gentleman of the prince's chamber (which post he owed to Calderon, whose creature he was supposed to be), afterwards so celebrated in the history of Philip IV. as Count of Olivarez and prime minister of Spain.

The conversation between Guzman and Uzeda, just before the Jesuit entered, was drawing to a close.

"You see," said Uzeda, "that if we desire to crush Calderon, it is on the Inquisition that we must depend. Now is the time to elect, in the successor of Sandoval y Roxas, one pledged to the favourite's ruin. The reason I choose Aliaga is this,—Calderon will never suspect his friendship, and will not, therefore, thwart us with the king. The Jesuit, who would sell all Christendom for the sake of advancement to his order or himself, will gladly sell Calderon to obtain the chair of the Inquisition."

"I believe it," replied Guzman. "I approve your choice; and you may rely on me to destroy Calderon with the prince. I have found out the way to rule Philip; it is by never giving him a right to despise his favourites,— it is to flatter his vanity, but not to share his vices. Trust me, you alone — if you follow my suggestions — can be minister to the Fourth Philip."

Here a page entered to announce Don Fray Louis d'Aliaga.

Uzeda advanced to the door, and received the holy man with profound respect.

"Be seated, father, and let me at once to business; for time presses, and all must be despatched to-night. Before interest is made by others with the king, we must be prompt in gaining the appointment of Sandoval's successor."

"Report says that the cardinal-duke, your father, himself desires the vacant chair of the Inquisition."

"My poor father, he is old,— his sun has set. No, Aliaga; I have thought of one fitter for that high and stern office: in a word, that appointment rests with yourself. I can make you Grand Inquisitor of Spain,— I."

"Me!" said the Jesuit, and he turned aside his face. "You jest with me, noble son."

"I am serious,— hear me. We have been foes and rivals; why should not our path be the same? Calderon has deprived you of friends more powerful than himself. His hour is come. The Duke de Lerma's downfall cannot be avoided; if it could, I, his son, would not, as you may suppose, withhold my hand. But business fatigues him; he is old; the affairs of Spain are in a deplorable condition; they need younger and abler hands. My father will not repine at a retirement suited to his years, and which shall be made honourable to his gray hairs. But some victim must glut the rage of the people; that victim must be the upstart Calderon; the means of his punishment, the Inquisition. Now, you understand me. On one condition you shall be the successor to Sandoval. Know that I do not promise without the power to fulfil. The instant I learned that the late cardinal's death was certain, I repaired to the king. I have the promise of the appointment; and this night your name shall, if you accept the condition, and Calderon does not in the interim see the king and prevent the nomination, receive the royal sanction."

"Our excellent Aliaga cannot hesitate," said Don Gaspar de Guzman. "The order of Loyola rests upon shoulders that can well support the load."

Before that trio separated, the compact was completed. Aliaga practised against his friend the lesson he had preached to him,— that the end sanctifies all means. Scarce had Aliaga departed ere Juan de la Nuza entered; for Uzeda, who sought to make the Inquisition his chief instrument of power, courted the friendship of all its officers. He readily promised to obtain the release of Fonseca; and, in effect, it was but little after midnight when an order arrived at the prison for the release of Don Martin de Fonseca, accompanied by a note from the duke to the prisoner, full of affectionate professions, and requesting to see him the next morning.

Late as the hour was, and in spite of the expostulations of the governor, who wished him to remain the night within the prison, in the hope to extract from him his secret, Fonseca no sooner received the order than he claimed and obtained his liberation.

----*----

CHAPTER X.

WE REAP WHAT WE SOW.

WITH emotions of joy and triumph, such as had never yet agitated his reckless and abandoned youth, the Infant of Spain bent his way towards the lonely house on the road to Fuencarral. He descended from his carriage when about a hundred yards from the abode, and proceeded on foot to the appointed place.

The Jew opened the door to the prince with a hideous grin on his hollow cheek; and Philip hastened up the stairs, and entering the chamber we have before described, beheld, to his inconceivable consternation and dismay, the form of Beatriz clasped in the arms of Calderon, her head leaning on his bosom, while his voice half choked with passionate sobs called upon her in the most endearing terms.

For a moment the prince stood, spell-bound and speechless, at the threshold; then, striking the hilt of his sword fiercely, he exclaimed, "Traitor! is it thus that thou hast kept thy promise? Dost thou not tremble at my vengeance?"

"Peace! peace!" said Calderon, in an imperious but sepulchral tone, and waving one hand with a gesture of impatience
and rebuke, while with the other he removed the long cluster-
ing hair that fell over the pale face of the still insensible
novice. "Peace, prince of Spain; thy voice scares back the
struggling life — peace! Look up, image and relic of the
lost, the murdered, the martyr! Hush! do you hear her
breathe, or is she with her mother in that heaven which is
closed on me? Live! live! my daughter, my child, live!
For thy life in the World Hereafter will *not* be mine!"

"What means this?" said the prince, falteringly. "What
delusion do thy wiles practise upon me?"

Calderon made no answer; and at that instant Beatriz
sighed heavily, and her eyes opened.

"My child! my child!—thou art my child! Speak! let
me hear thy voice; again let it call me 'father'!"

And Calderon dropped on his knees, and, clasping his
hands fervently, looked up imploringly in her face. The
novice, now slowly returning to life and consciousness, strove
to speak; her voice failed her, but her lips smiled upon
Calderon, and her arms fell feebly but endearingly round his
neck.

"Bless thee! bless thee!" exclaimed Calderon. "Bless
thee in thy sweet mother's name!"

While he spoke the eyes of Beatriz caught the form of
Philip, who stood by, leaning on his sword, his face working
with various passions, and his lip curling with stern and in-
tense disdain. Accustomed to know human life but in its
worst shapes, and Calderon only by his vices and his arts,
the voice of nature uttered no language intelligible to the
prince. He regarded the whole as some well got-up device,
— some trick of the stage; and waited, with impatience and
scorn, the *dénouement* of the imposture.

At the sight of that mocking face, Beatriz shuddered, and
fell back; but her very alarm revived her, and starting to her
feet, she exclaimed, "Save me from that bad man,— save me!
My father, I *am* safe with thee!"

"Safe!" echoed Calderon,— "ay, safe against the world.

But not," he added, looking round, and in a low and muttered tone, "not in this foul abode; its very air pollutes thee. Let us hence: come, come, my daughter!" and winding his arm round her waist, he hurried her towards the door.

"Back, traitor!" cried Philip, placing himself full in the path of the distracted and half delirious father. "Back! thinkest thou that I, thy master and thy prince, am to be thus duped and thus insulted? Not for thine own pleasures hast thou snatched her whom I have honoured with my love from the sanctuary of the Church. Go, if thou wilt; but Beatriz remains. This roof is sacred to my will. Back! or thy next step is on the point of my sword."

"Menace not, speak not, Philip,— I am desperate. I am beside myself, I cannot parley with thee. Away! by thy hopes of Heaven, away! I am no longer thy minion, thy tool. I am a father, and the protector of my child."

"Brave device! notable tale!" cried Philip, scornfully, and placing his back against the door. "The little actress plays her part well, it must be owned,— it is her trade; but thou art a bungler, my gentle Calderon."

For a moment the courtier stood, not irresolute, but overcome with the passions that shook to their centre a nature, the stormy and stern elements of which the habit of years had rather mastered than quelled. At last, with a fierce cry, he suddenly grasped the prince by the collar of his vest; and, ere Philip could avail himself of his weapon, swung him aside with such violence that he lost his balance and (his foot slipping on the polished floor) fell to the ground. Calderon then opened the door, lifted Beatriz in both his arms, and fled precipitately down the stairs. He could no longer trust to chance and delay against the dangers of that abode.

CHAPTER XI.

HOWSOEVER THE RIVERS WIND, THE OCEAN RECEIVES THEM
ALL.

MEANWHILE Fonseca had reached the convent; had found
the porter gone; and, with a mind convulsed with apprehen-
sion and doubt, had flown on the wings of love and fear to
the house indicated by Calderon.   The grim and solitary
mansion came just in sight — the moon streaming sadly over
its gray and antique walls — when he heard his name pronounced, and the convent porter emerged from the shadow of
a wall beside which he had ensconced himself.

"Don Martin! it is thou indeed; blessed be the saints !   I
began to fear,— nay, I fear now, that we were deceived."

"Speak, man, but stop me not !   Speak ! what horrors hast
thou to utter? "

"I knew the cavalier whom thou didst send in thy place !
Who knows not Roderigo Calderon?   I trembled when I saw
him lift the novice into the carriage; but I thought I should,
as agreed, be companion in the flight.   Not so.   Don Roderigo
briefly told me to hide where I could this night; and that
to-morrow he would arrange preparations for my flight from
Madrid.   My mind misgave me, for Calderon's name is black-
ened by many curses.   I resolved to follow the carriage.   I
did so; but my breath and speed nearly failed, when, fortu-
nately, the carriage was stopped and entangled by a crowd in
the street.   No lackeys were behind; I mounted the foot-
board unobserved, and descended and hid myself when the
carriage stopped.   I knew not the house, but I knew the
neighbourhood — a brother of mine lives at hand.   I sought
my relative for a night's shelter.   I learned that dark stories
had given to that house an evil name.   It was one of those
which the Prince of Spain had consecrated to the pursuits

that have dishonoured so many families in Madrid. I resolved again to go forth and watch. Scarce had I reached this very spot when I saw a carriage approach rapidly. I secreted myself behind a buttress, and saw the carriage halt; and a man descended, and walked to the house. See there — there, by yon crossing, the carriage still waits. The man was wrapped in a mantle. I know not whom he may be; but — "

"Heavens!" cried Fonseca, as they were now close before the door of the house at which Calderon's carriage still stood; "I hear a noise, a shriek, within."

Scarce had he spoken when the door opened. Voices were heard in loud altercation; presently the form of the Jew was thrown on the pavement, and dashing aside another man, who seemed striving to detain him, Calderon appeared,— his drawn sword in his right hand, his left arm clasped round Beatriz.

Fonseca darted forward.

"My lover! my betrothed!" exclaimed the voice of the novice; "thou art come to save us,— to save thy Beatriz!"

"Yes; and to chastise the betrayer!" exclaimed Fonseca in a voice of thunder. "Leave thy victim, villain! Defend thyself!"

He made a desperate lunge at Calderon while he spoke. The marquis feebly parried the stroke.

"Hold!" he cried. "Not on me!"

"No! no!" exclaimed Beatriz, throwing herself on her father's breast. The words came too late. Blinded and deafened with rage, Fonseca had again, with more sure and deadly aim, directed his weapon against his supposed foe. The blade struck home, but not to the heart of Calderon. It was Beatriz, bathed in her blood, who fell at the feet of her frenzied lover.

"Daughter and mother both!" muttered Calderon; and he fell as if the steel had pierced his own heart, beside his child.

"Wretch! what hast thou done?" muttered a voice strange to the ear of Fonseca,— a voice half stifled with horror and, perhaps, remorse. The Prince of Spain stood on the spot, and his feet were dabbled in the blood of the virgin martyr. The moonlight alone lighted that spectacle of crime and death; and the faces of all seemed ghastly beneath its beams. Beatriz turned her eyes upon her lover, with an expression of celestial compassion, and divine forgiveness; then sinking upon Calderon's breast, she muttered,—

"Pardon him! pardon him, Father! I shall tell my mother that thou hast blessed me!"

.   .   .   .

It was not for several days after that night of terror that Calderon was heard of at the court. His absence was unaccountable; for, though the flight of the novice was of course known, her fate was not suspected; and her rank had been too insignificant to create much interest in her escape or much vigilance in pursuit. But of that absence the courtier's enemies well availed themselves. The plans of the cabal were ripe; and the aid of the Inquisition, by the appointment of Aliaga, was added to the machinations of Uzeda's partisans. The king was deeply incensed at the mysterious absence of Calderon, for which a thousand ingenious conjectures were invented. The Duke of Lerma, infirm and enfeebled by years, was unable to confront his foes. With imbecile despair he called on the name of Calderon; and when no trace of that powerful ally could be discovered, he forbore even to seek an interview with the king. Suddenly the storm broke. One evening Lérma received the royal order to surrender his posts, and to quit the court by daybreak. It was in this very hour that the door of Lerma's chamber opened, and Roderigo Calderon stood before him. But how changed! how blasted from his former self! His eyes were sunk deep in their sockets, and their fire was quenched; his cheeks were hollow, his frame bent, and when he spoke his voice was as that of one calling from the tomb.

"Behold me, Duke de Lerma, I am returned at last!"

"Returned — blessings on thee! Where hast thou been? Why didst thou desert me? — no matter, thou art returned! Fly to the king,— tell him I am not old! I do not want repose. Defeat the villany of my unnatural son! They would

banish me, Calderon,—banish me in the very prime of my
years! My son says I am old—old!—ha! ha! Fly to the
prince; he too has immured himself in his apartment. He
would not see me; he will see *thee!*"

"Ay, the prince! we have cause to love each other!"

"Ye have indeed! Hasten, Calderon; not a moment is to
be lost! Banished! Calderon, *shall* I be banished?" And
the old man, bursting into tears, fell at the feet of Calderon,
and clasped his knees. "Go, go, I implore thee! Save me;
I loved *thee*, Calderon, I always loved thee. Shall our foes
triumph? Shall the horn of the wicked be exalted?"

For a moment (so great is the mechanical power of habit)
there returned to Calderon something of his wonted energy
and spirit; a light broke from his sunken eyes; he drew himself up to the full of his stately height. "I thought I had
done with courts and with life," said he; "but I will make
one more effort; I will not forsake you in your hour of need.
Yes, Uzeda shall be baffled; I will seek the king. Fear not,
my lord, fear not; the charm of my power is not yet broken."

So saying, Calderon raised the cardinal from the ground,
and extricating himself from the old man's grasp strode,
with his customary air of majestic self-reliance, to the door.
Just ere he reached it, three low but regular knocks sounded
on the panel; the door opened, and the space without was
filled with the dark forms of the officers of the Inquisition.

"Stand!" said a deep voice; "stand, Roderigo Calderon,
Marquis de Siete Iglesias; in the name of the most Holy
Inquisition, we arrest thee!"

"Aliaga!" muttered Calderon, falling back.

"Peace!" interrupted the Jesuit. "Officers, remove your
prisoner."

"Poor old man," said Calderon, turning towards the cardinal, who stood spell-bound and speechless, "*thy* life at least
is safe. For me, I defy fate! Lead on!"

The Prince of Spain soon recovered from the shock which
the death of Beatriz at first occasioned him. New pleasures
chased away even remorse. He appeared again in public a

few days after the arrest of Calderon; and he made strong intercession on behalf of his former favourite. But even had the Inquisition desired to relax its grasp, or Uzeda to forego his vengeance, so great was the exultation of the people at the fall of the dreaded and obnoxious secretary, and so numerous the charges which party malignity added to those which truth could lay at his door, that it would have required a far bolder monarch than Philip the Third to have braved the voice of a whole nation for the sake of a disgraced minister. The prince himself was soon induced by new favourites to consider any further interference on his part equally impolitic and vain; and the Duke d'Uzeda and Don Gaspar de Guzman were minions quite as supple, while they were companions infinitely more respectable.

One day, an officer, attending the levee of the prince, with whom he was a special favourite, presented a memorial requesting the interest of his highness for an appointment in the royal armies, that, he had just learned by an express, was vacant.

"And whose death comes so opportunely for thy rise, Don Alvar?" asked the Infant.

"Don Martin Fonseca.   He fell in the late skirmish, pierced by a hundred wounds."

The prince started and turned hastily away. The officer lost all favour from that hour, and never learned his offence.

Meanwhile months passed, and Calderon still languished in his dungeon. At last the Inquisition opened against him its dark register of accusations. First of these charges was that of sorcery, practised on the king; the rest were for the most part equally grotesque and extravagant. These accusations Calderon met with a dignity which confounded his foes, and belied the popular belief in the elements of his character. Submitted to the rack, he bore its tortures without a groan; and all historians have accorded concurrent testimony to the patience and heroism which characterized the close of his wild and meteoric career.

At length Philip the Third died; the Infant ascended the throne,— that prince, for whom the ambitious courtier had perilled alike life and soul! The people now believed that they should be defrauded of their victim. They were mistaken. The new king, by this time, had forgotten even the existence of the favourite of the prince. But Guzman, who, while affecting to minister to the interests of Uzeda, was secretly aiming at the monopoly of the royal favour, felt himself insecure while Calderon yet lived. The operations of the Inquisition were too slow for the impatience of his fears; and as that dread tribunal affected never to inflict death until the accused had confessed his guilt, the firmness of Calderon baffled the vengeance of the ecclesiastical law. New inquiries were set on foot; a corpse was discovered, buried in Calderon's garden,— the corpse of a female. He was accused of the murder. Upon that charge he was transferred from the Inquisition to the regular courts of justice. No evidence could be produced against him; but, to the astonishment of all, he made no defence, and his silence was held the witness of his crime. He was adjudged to the scaffold — he smiled when he heard the sentence.

An immense crowd, one bright day in summer, were assembled in the place of execution. A shout of savage exultation rent the air as Roderigo Calderon, Marquis de Siete Iglesias, appeared upon the scaffold. But, when the eyes of the multitude rested — not upon that lofty and stately form, in all the pride of manhood, which they had been accustomed to associate with their fears of the stern genius and iron power of the favourite — but upon a bent and spectral figure, that seemed already on the verge of a natural grave, with a face ploughed deep with traces of unutterable woe, and hollow eyes that looked with dim and scarce conscious light over the human sea that murmured and swayed below, the tide of the popular emotion changed; to rage and triumph succeeded shame and pity. Not a hand was lifted up in accusation,— not a voice was raised in rebuke or joy. Beside Calderon stood the appointed priest, whispering cheer and consolation.

"Fear not, my son," said the holy man   "The pang of the body strikes years of purgatory from thy doom. Think of this, and bless even the agony of this hour."

"Yes," muttered Calderon; "I do bless this hour. Inez, thy daughter has avenged thy murder! May Heaven accept the sacrifice! and may my eyes, even athwart the fiery gulf, awaken upon thee!"

With that a serene and contented smile passed over the face on which the crowd gazed with breathless awe. A minute more, and a groan, a cry, broke from that countless multitude; and a gory and ghastly head, severed from its trunk, was raised on high.

Two spectators of that execution were in one of the balconies that commanded a full view of its terrors.

"So perishes my worst foe!" said Uzeda.

"We must sacrifice all things, friends as foes, in the ruthless march of the Great Cause," rejoined the Grand Inquisitor; but he sighed as he spoke.

"Guzman is now with the king," said Uzeda, turning into the chamber. "I expect every instant a summons into the royal presence."

"I cannot share thy sanguine hopes, my son," said Aliaga, shaking his head. "My profession has made me a deep reader of human character. Gaspar de Guzman will remove every rival from his path."

While he spoke, there entered a gentleman of the royal chamber. He presented to the Grand Inquisitor and the expectant duke two letters signed by the royal hand. They were the mandates of banishment and disgrace. Not even the ghostly rank of the Grand Inquisitor, not even the profound manœuvres of the son of Lerma, availed them against the vigilance and vigour of the new favourite. Simultaneously, a shout from the changeable crowd below proclaimed that the king's choice of his new minister was published and approved.

And Aliaga and Uzeda exchanged glances that bespoke all the passions that make defeated ambition the worst fiend, as they heard the mighty cry, "Long live Olivarez the Reformer!"

That cry came, faint and muffled, to the ears of Philip the Fourth, as he sat in his palace with his new minister.

"Whence that shout?" said the king, hastily.

"It rises, doubtless, from the honest hearts of your loyal people at the execution of Calderon."

Philip shaded his face with his hand, and mused a moment; then, turning to Olivarez with a sarcastic smile, he said: "Behold the moral of the life of a courtier, Count! What do they say of the new opera?"

At the close of his life, in disgrace and banishment, the count-duke, for the first time since they had been uttered, called to his recollection those words of his royal master.[1]

---

[1] The fate of Calderon has given rise to many tales and legends. Amongst those who have best availed themselves of so fruitful a subject may be ranked the late versatile and ingenious Telesforo de Trueba, in his work on "The Romances of Spain." In a few of the incidents, and in some of the names, his sketch, called "The Fortunes of Calderon," has a resemblance to the story just concluded. The plot, characters, and principal events are, however, widely distinct in our several adaptations of an ambiguous and unsatisfactory portion of Spanish history.

THE END.

.

www.ingramcontent.com/pod-product-compliance
Lightning Source LLC
Chambersburg PA
CBHW020008290326
41935CB00007B/349